HEROIC ANIMALS
MOKO TO THE RESCUE
HEROIC DOLPHIN OF NEW ZEALAND

BY **MATTHEW K. MANNING**   ILLUSTRATED BY **DOLO OKĘCKI**

CAPSTONE PRESS
a capstone imprint

Published by Capstone Press, an imprint of Capstone.
1710 Roe Crest Drive, North Mankato, Minnesota 56003
capstonepub.com

Library of Congress Cataloging-in-Publication Data
Names: Manning, Matthew K., author. | Okęcki, Dolo, illustrator.
Title: Moko to the rescue : heroic dolphin of New Zealand /
  by Matthew K. Manning ; illustrated by Dolo Okecki.
Description: North Mankato, Minnesota : Capstone Press, an imprint
  of Capstone, [2023] | Series: Heroic animals | Includes bibliographical
  references. | Audience: Ages 8-11 | Audience: Grades 4-6
Summary: "In 2008, Moko the dolphin was well known at Mahia Beach on New Zealand's North
  Island. People loved to come and watch the playful dolphin fetch beach balls, steal boogie
  boards, and interact with the swimmers and beachgoers. In March of that year, two pygmy
  sperm whales got trapped between a sandbar and the beach and couldn't get them back to the
  ocean. Several concerned people were unable to help the whales-until Moko came along. Dive
  in and learn all about the heroic dolphin who helped lead two distressed whales back to the
  safety of the sea"—Provided by publisher.
Identifiers: LCCN 2022024616 (print) | LCCN 2022024617 (ebook) |
  ISBN 9781666393965 (hardcover) | ISBN 9781666394092 (paperback) |
  ISBN 9781666393958 (ebook PDF) | ISBN 9781666394115 (kindle edition)
Subjects: LCSH: Dolphins--New Zealand--Anecdotes--Juvenile literature. |
  Dolphins—Effect of human beings on—New Zealand—Juvenile literature. |
  Human-animal relationships—New Zealand—Juvenile literature.
Classification: LCC QL795.D7 M36 2023 (print) | LCC QL795.D7 (ebook) |
  DDC 599.530993—dc23/eng/20220630
LC record available at https://lccn.loc.gov/2022024616
LC ebook record available at https://lccn.loc.gov/2022024617

Editorial Credits
Editor: Aaron Sautter; Designer: Elyse White; Media Researcher: Donna Metcalf;
Production Specialist: Tori Abraham

Photo Credit
Associated Press/ Gisborne Herald, 29

All internet sites appearing in back matter were available and accurate when this book was sent
to press.

Direct quotes appear in **bold, italicized** text on the following pages:

Page 17: from Moko the dolphin helps locals save whales from beaching, by NZPA. Nzherald.
  co.nz, 2008, https://www.nzherald.co.nz/nz/moko-the-dolphin-helps-locals-save-whales-
  from-beaching/GJV57EO3M7ETDFOPX4X5BZL3VA/
Page 18: from 60 Minutes: Loved To Death. New Zealand: 2011, https://www.youtube.com/
  watch?v=bscf8vp75PI
Page 21: from NZ dolphin rescues beached whales, BBC News. News.bbc.co.uk, 2008,
  http://news.bbc.co.uk/1/hi/world/asia-pacific/7291501.stm
Page 23: from Save the whales: How Moko the dolphin came to the rescue of a mother and her
  calf, by Kathy Marks. Independent.com.uk, 2008, https://www.independent.co.uk/climate-
  change/news/save-the-whales-how-moko-the-dolphin-came-to-the-rescue-of-a-mother-and-
  her-calf-795025.html

Printed and bound in the USA.   PO# 5195

TABLE OF CONTENTS

Chapter 1: Family Lost 4

Chapter 2: Beach Life 6

Chapter 3: Trouble at the Beach 12

Chapter 4: Moko to the Rescue........ 18

Chapter 5: New Families Found 26

Moko's Amazing Life 29
Glossary 30
Internet Sites............................31
Read More 31
About the Author......................32
About the Illustrator 32

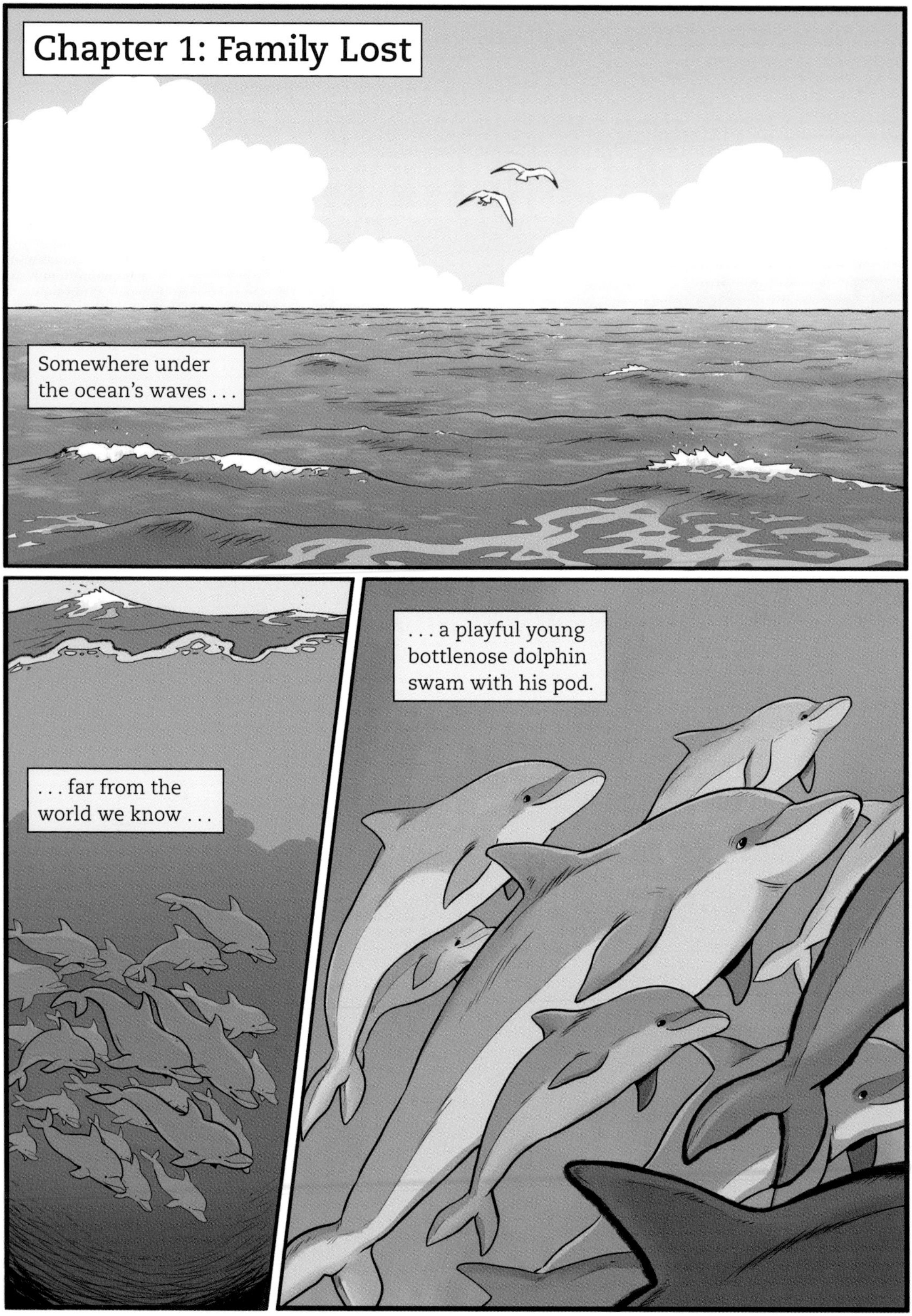
Chapter 1: Family Lost
Somewhere under the ocean's waves . . .
. . . far from the world we know . . .
. . . a playful young bottlenose dolphin swam with his pod.

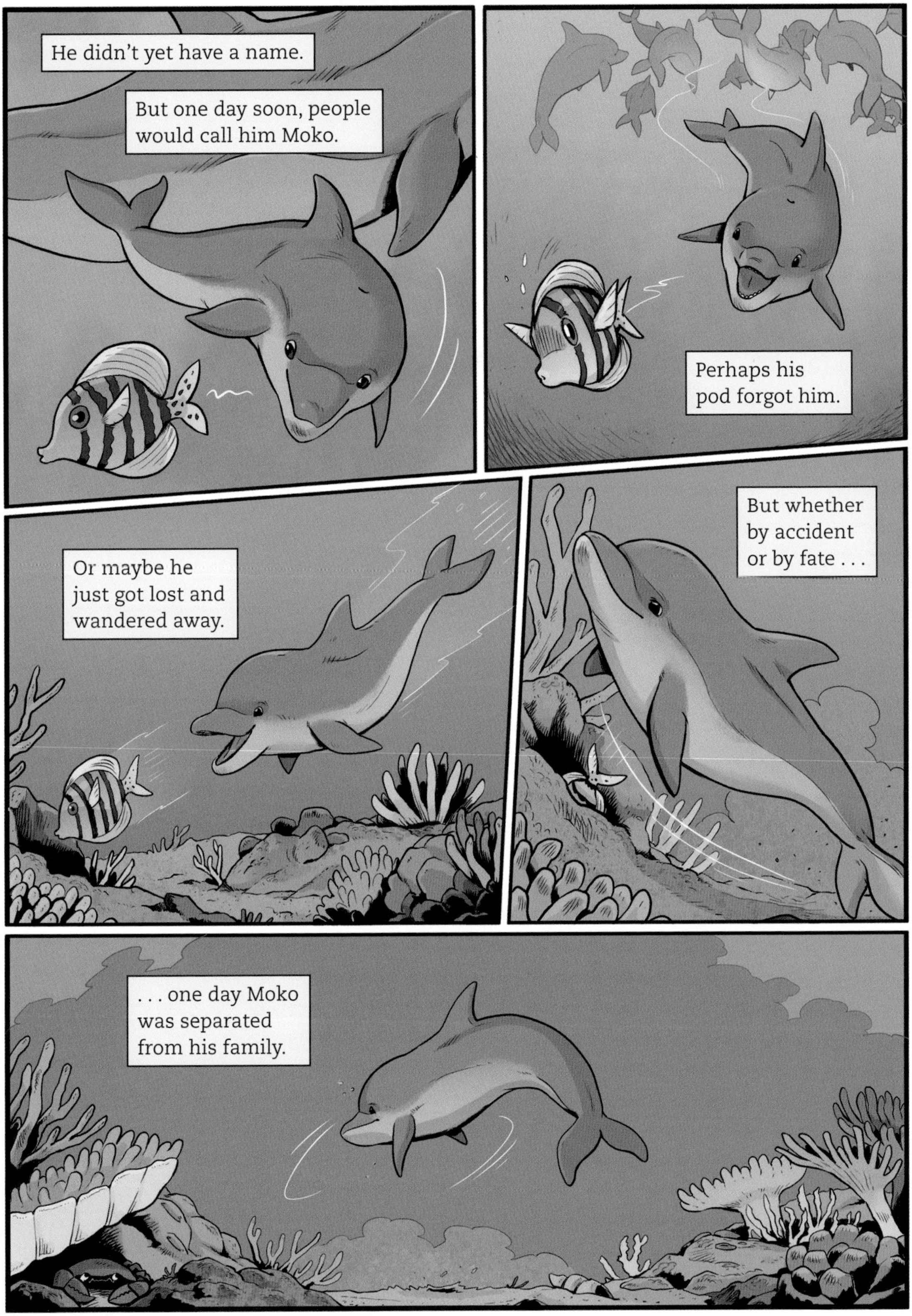
He didn't yet have a name.
But one day soon, people would call him Moko.
Perhaps his pod forgot him.
Or maybe he just got lost and wandered away.
But whether by accident or by fate . . .
. . . one day Moko was separated from his family.

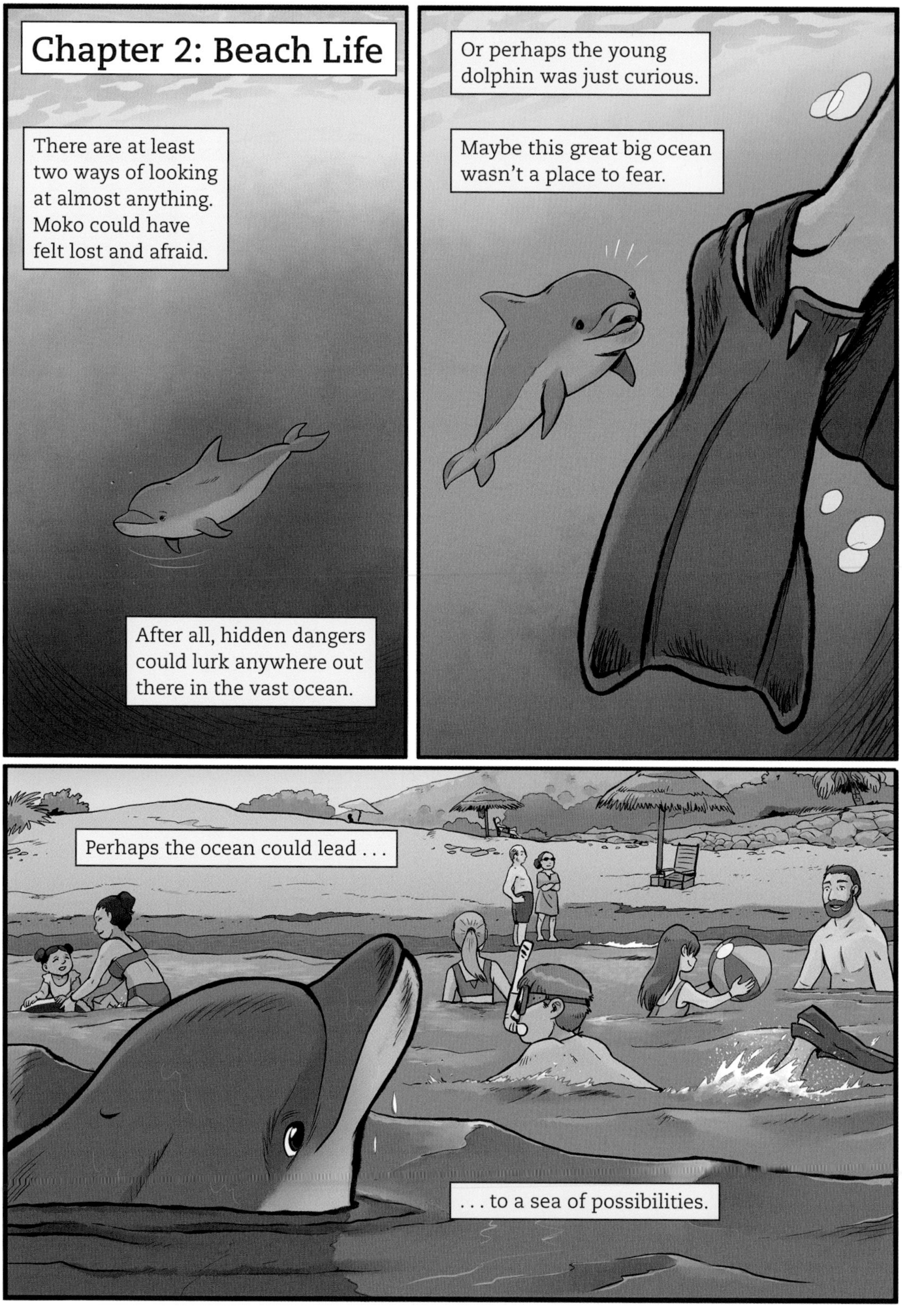
Chapter 2: Beach Life
There are at least two ways of looking at almost anything. Moko could have felt lost and afraid.
After all, hidden dangers could lurk anywhere out there in the vast ocean.
Or perhaps the young dolphin was just curious.
Maybe this great big ocean wasn't a place to fear.
Perhaps the ocean could lead . . .
. . . to a sea of possibilities.

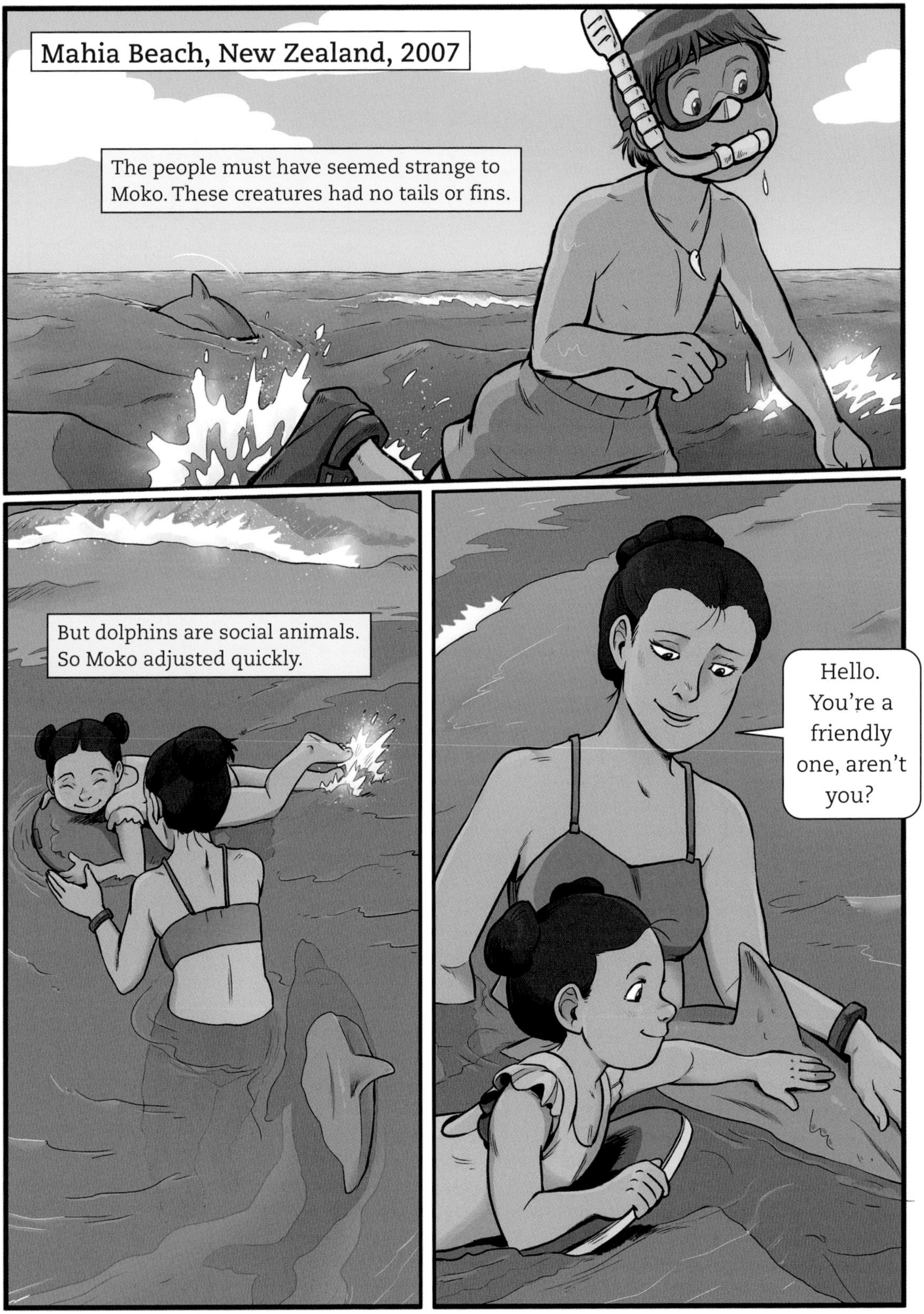
Mahia Beach, New Zealand, 2007
The people must have seemed strange to Moko. These creatures had no tails or fins.
But dolphins are social animals. So Moko adjusted quickly.
Hello. You're a friendly one, aren't you?

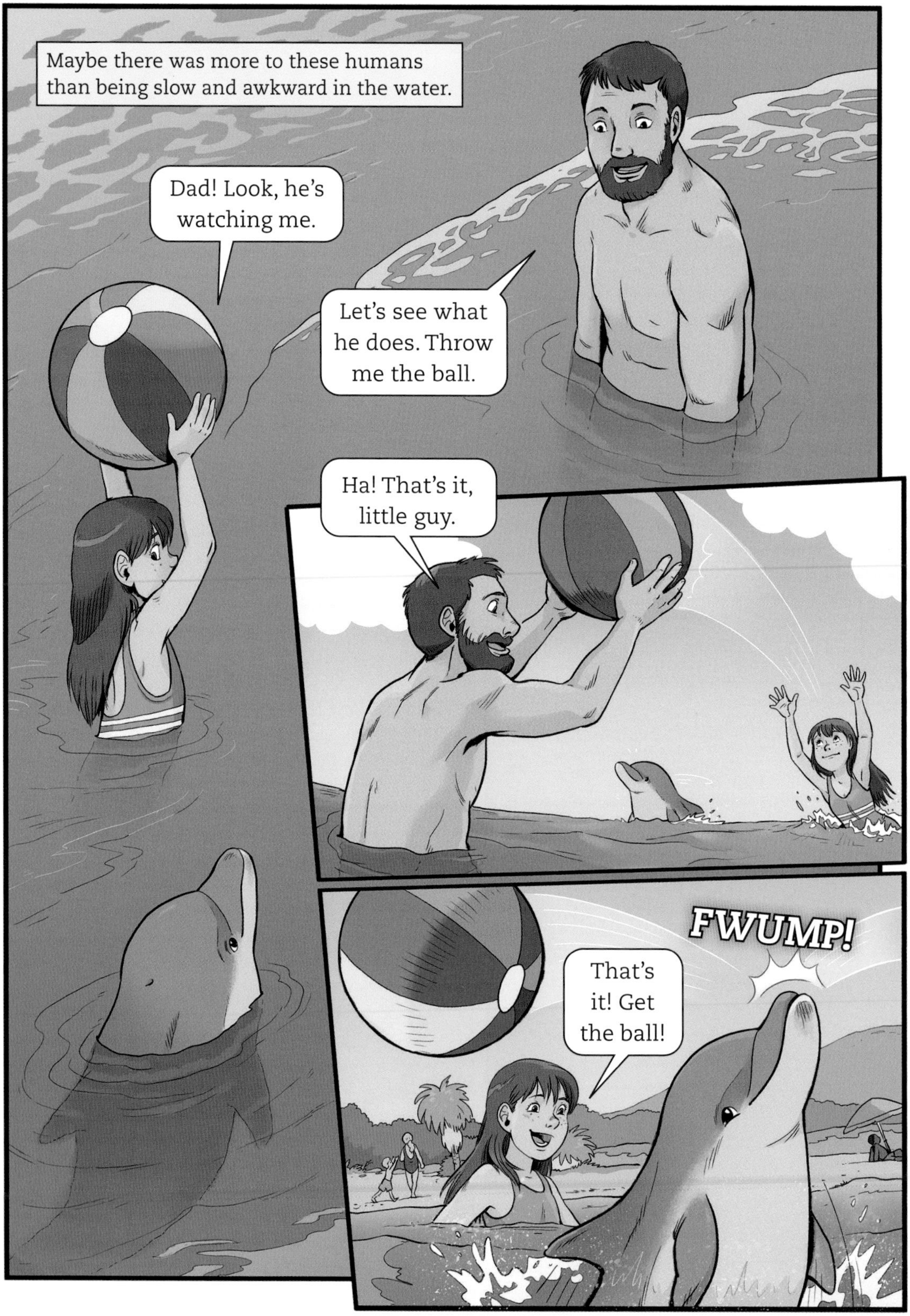
Maybe there was more to these humans than being slow and awkward in the water.
Dad! Look, he's watching me.
Let's see what he does. Throw me the ball.
Ha! That's it, little guy.
FWUMP!
That's it! Get the ball!

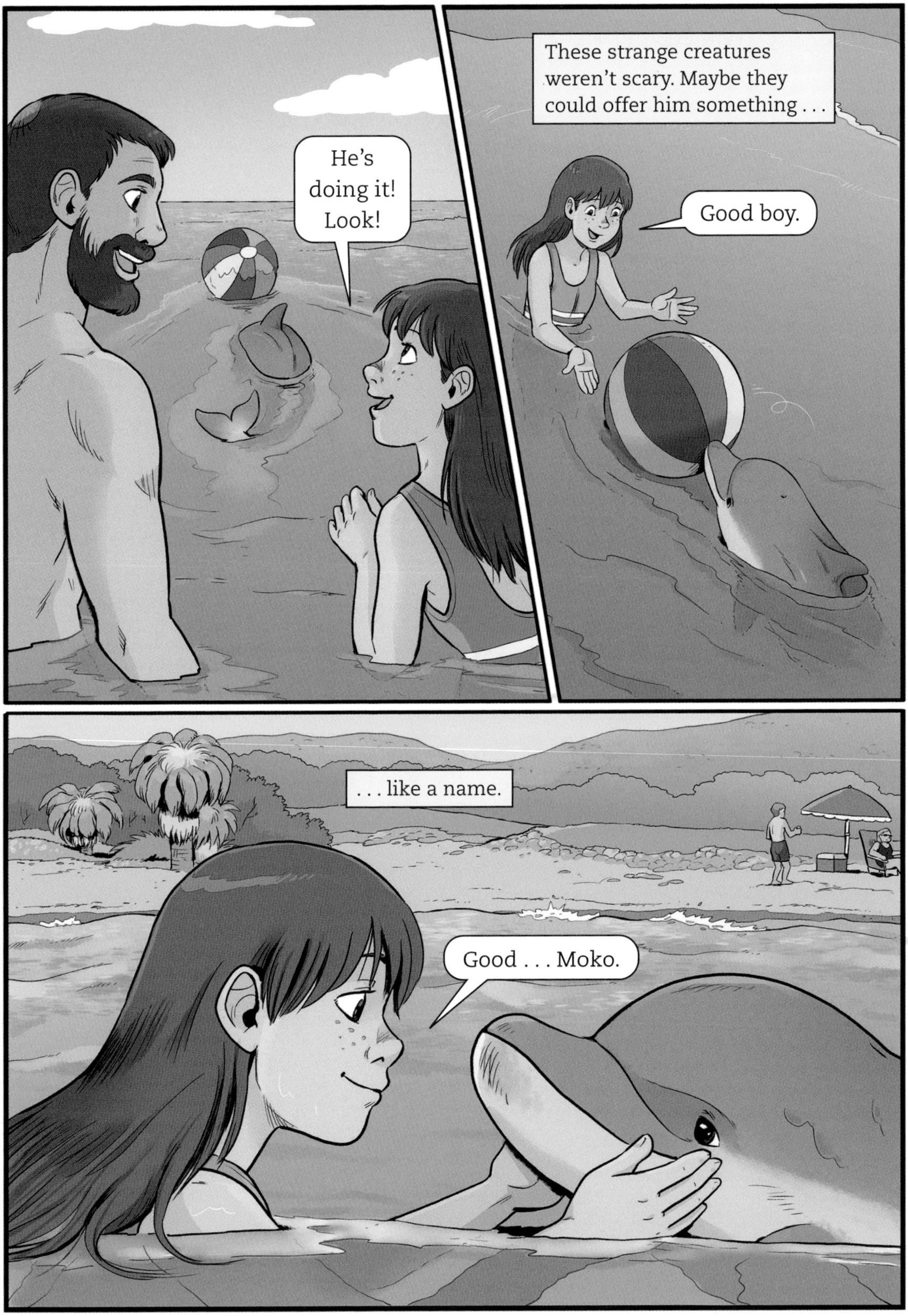
He's doing it! Look!
These strange creatures weren't scary. Maybe they could offer him something . . .
Good boy.
. . . like a name.
Good . . . Moko.

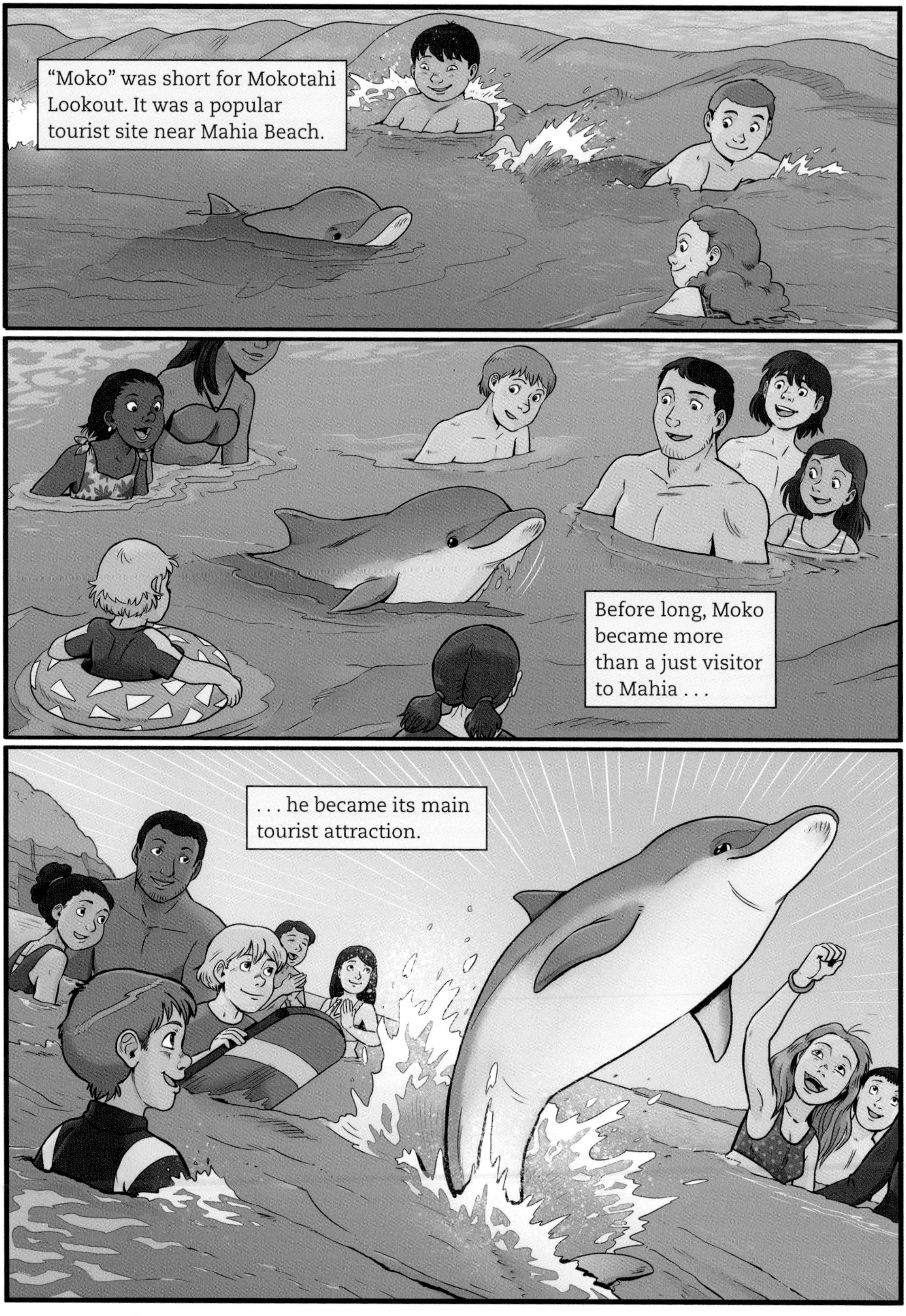
"Moko" was short for Mokotahi Lookout. It was a popular tourist site near Mahia Beach.
Before long, Moko became more than a just visitor to Mahia . . .
. . . he became its main tourist attraction.

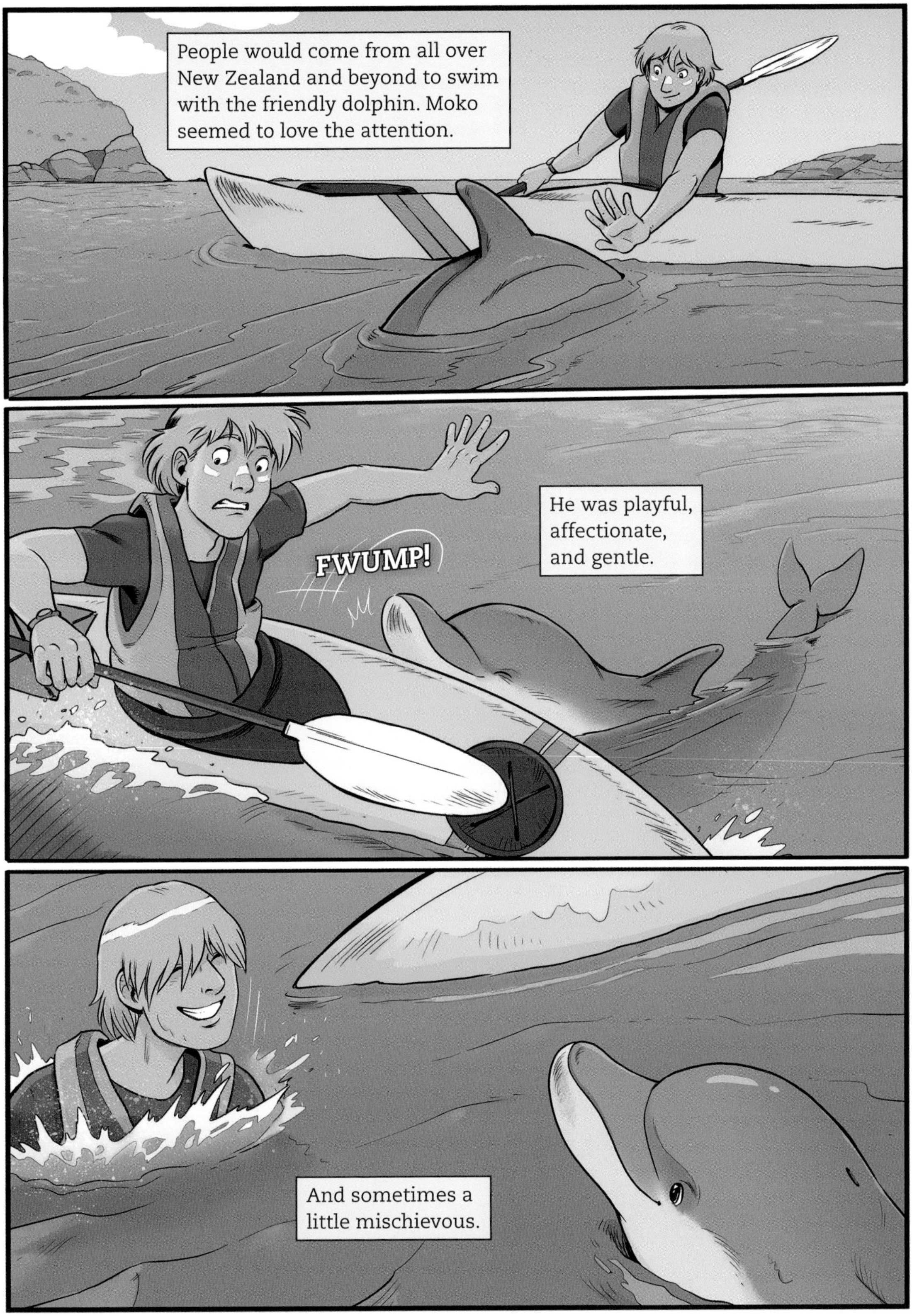
People would come from all over New Zealand and beyond to swim with the friendly dolphin. Moko seemed to love the attention.
He was playful, affectionate, and gentle.
FWUMP!
And sometimes a little mischievous.

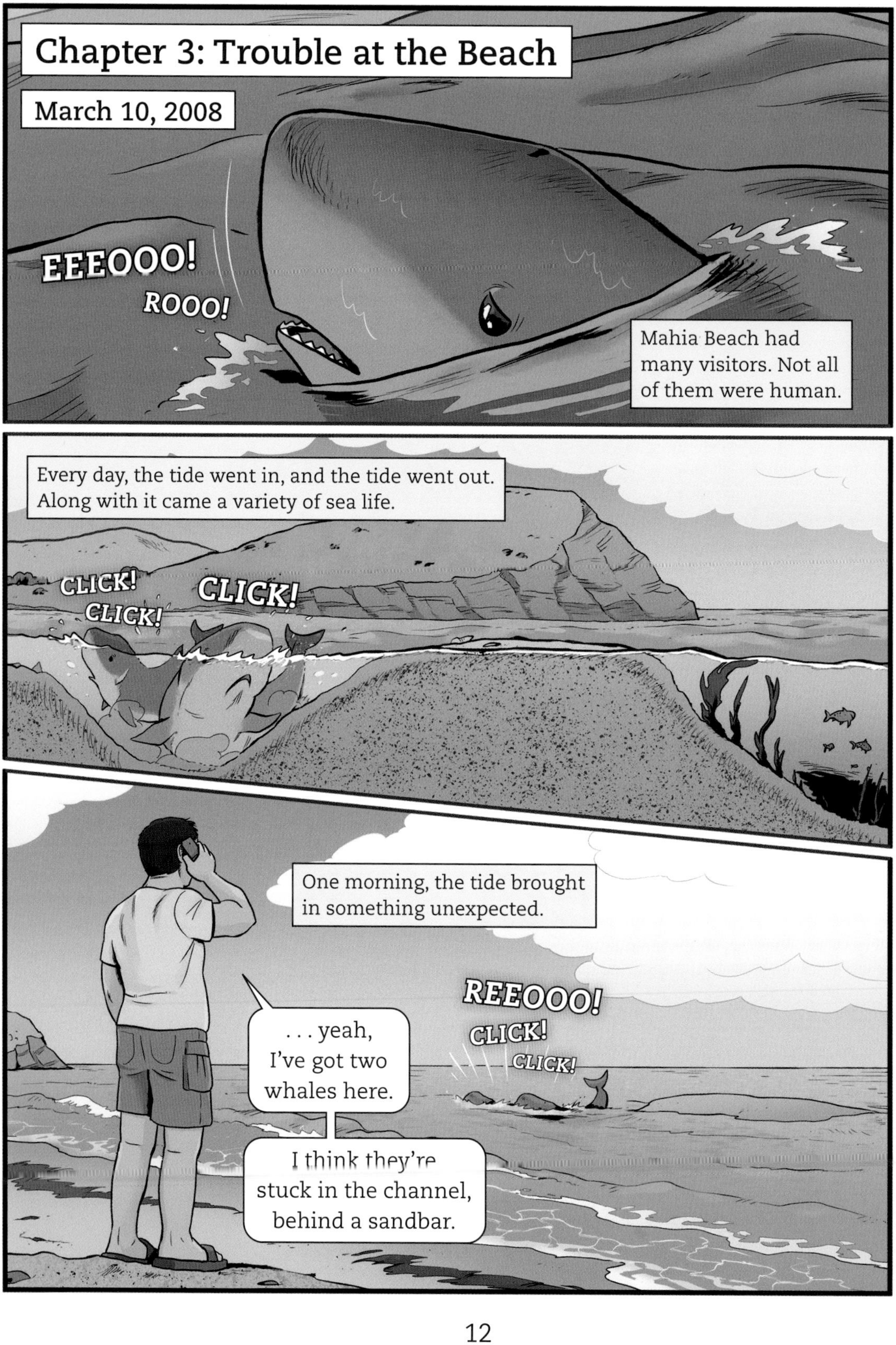
Chapter 3: Trouble at the Beach
March 10, 2008
EEEOOO!
ROOO!
Mahia Beach had many visitors. Not all of them were human.
Every day, the tide went in, and the tide went out. Along with it came a variety of sea life.
CLICK!
CLICK!
CLICK!
One morning, the tide brought in something unexpected.
. . . yeah, I've got two whales here.
I think they're stuck in the channel, behind a sandbar.
REEOOO!
CLICK!
CLICK!

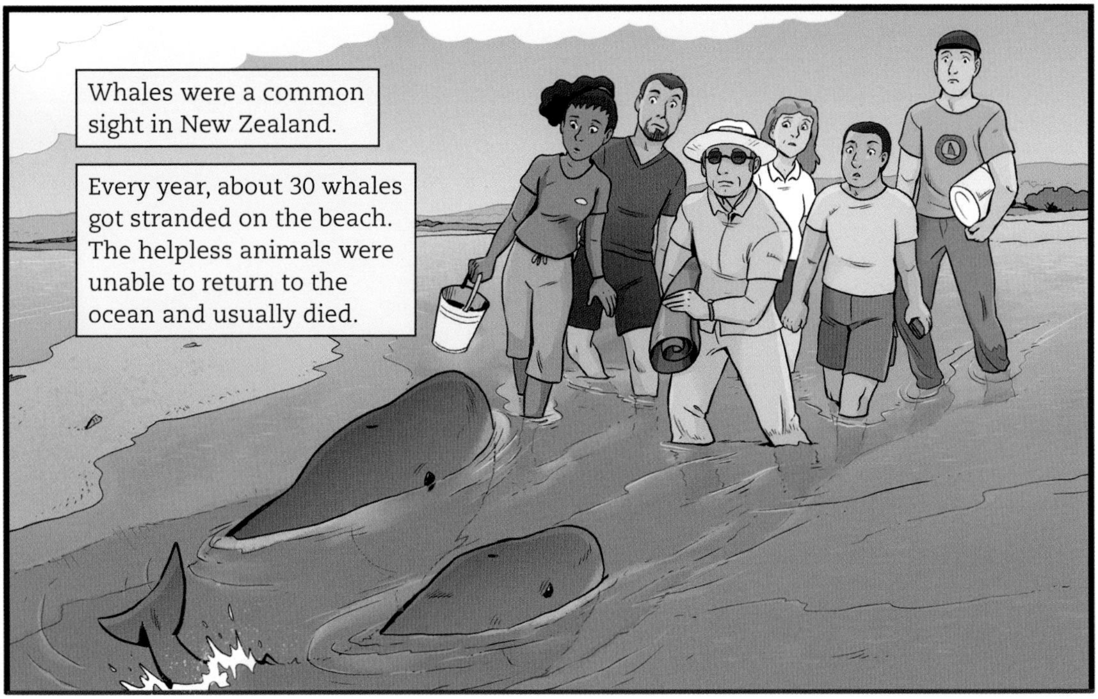
Whales were a common sight in New Zealand.
Every year, about 30 whales got stranded on the beach. The helpless animals were unable to return to the ocean and usually died.

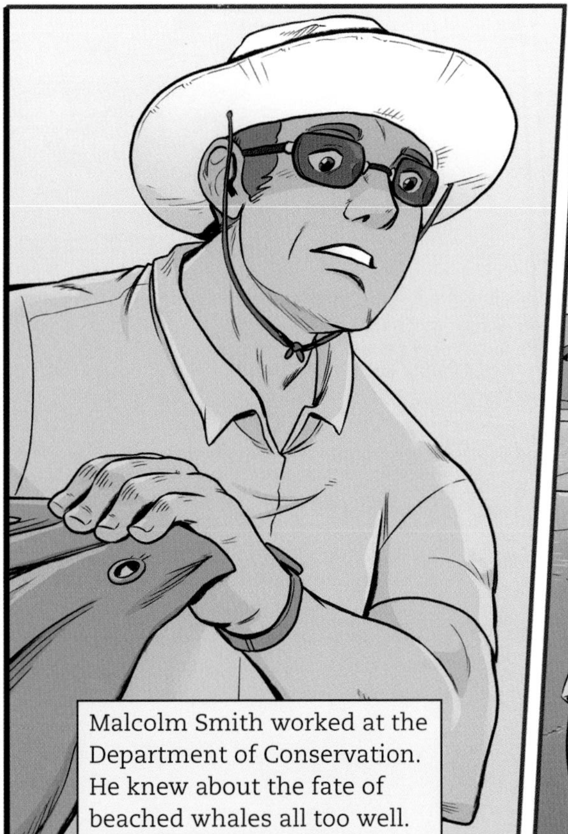
Malcolm Smith worked at the Department of Conservation. He knew about the fate of beached whales all too well.

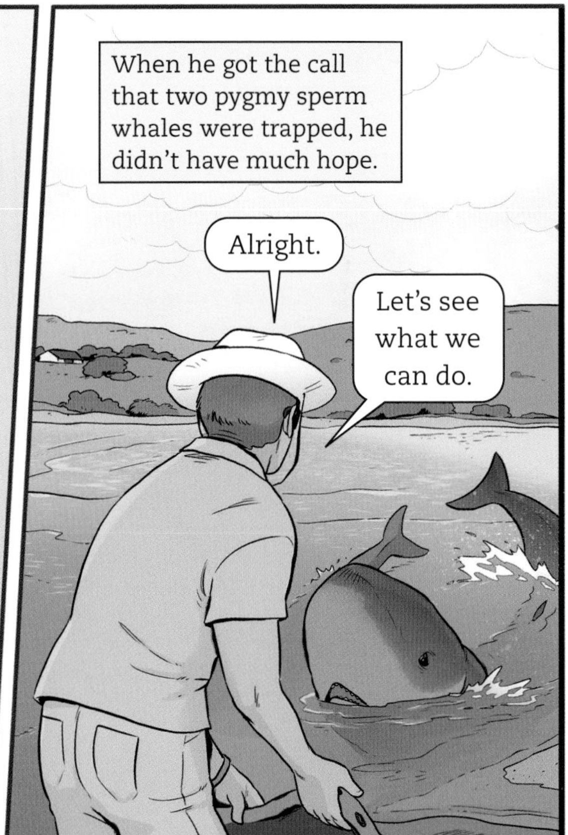
When he got the call that two pygmy sperm whales were trapped, he didn't have much hope.
Alright.
Let's see what we can do.

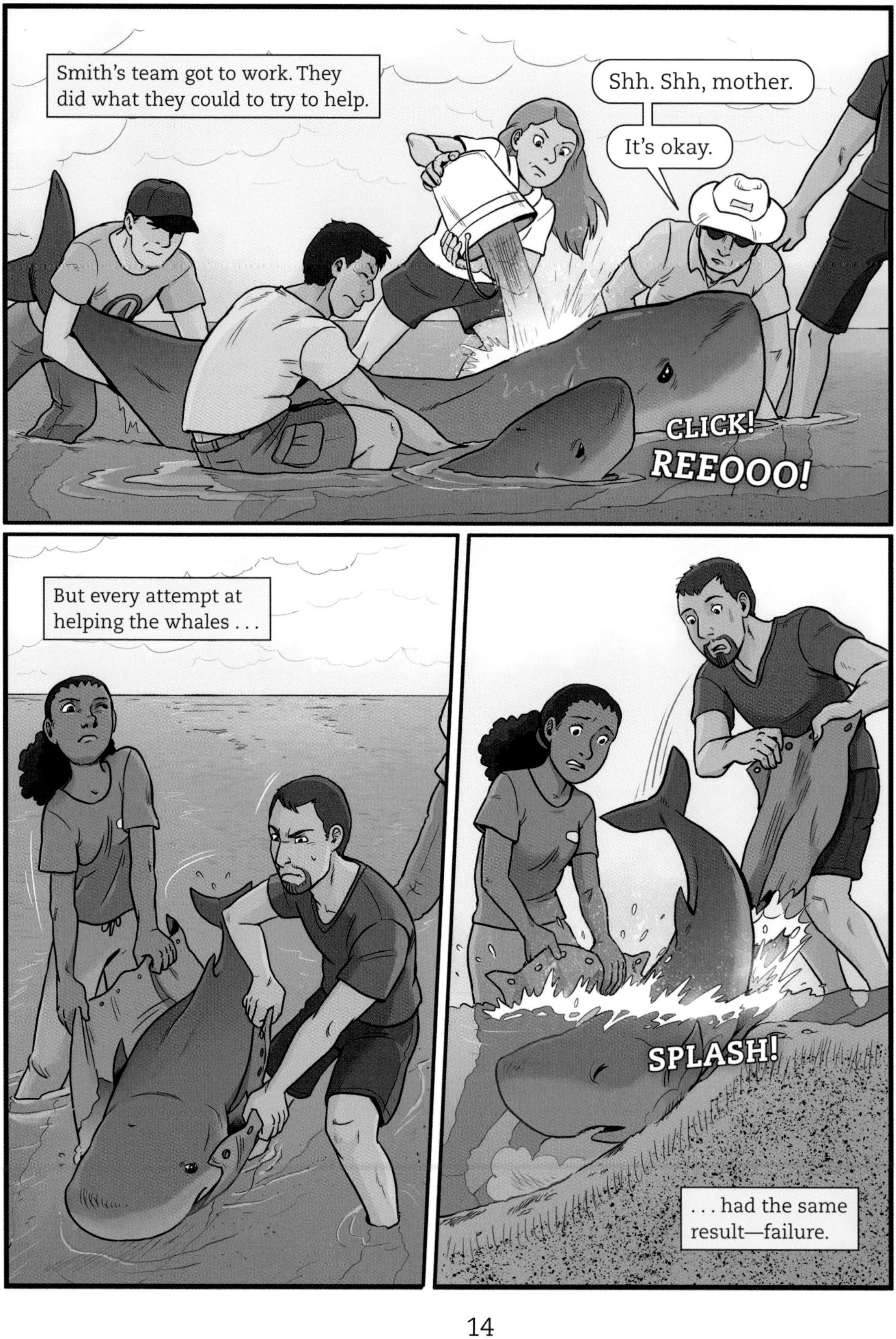
Smith's team got to work. They did what they could to try to help.
Shh. Shh, mother.
It's okay.
CLICK!
REEOOO!
But every attempt at helping the whales . . .
SPLASH!
. . . had the same result—failure.

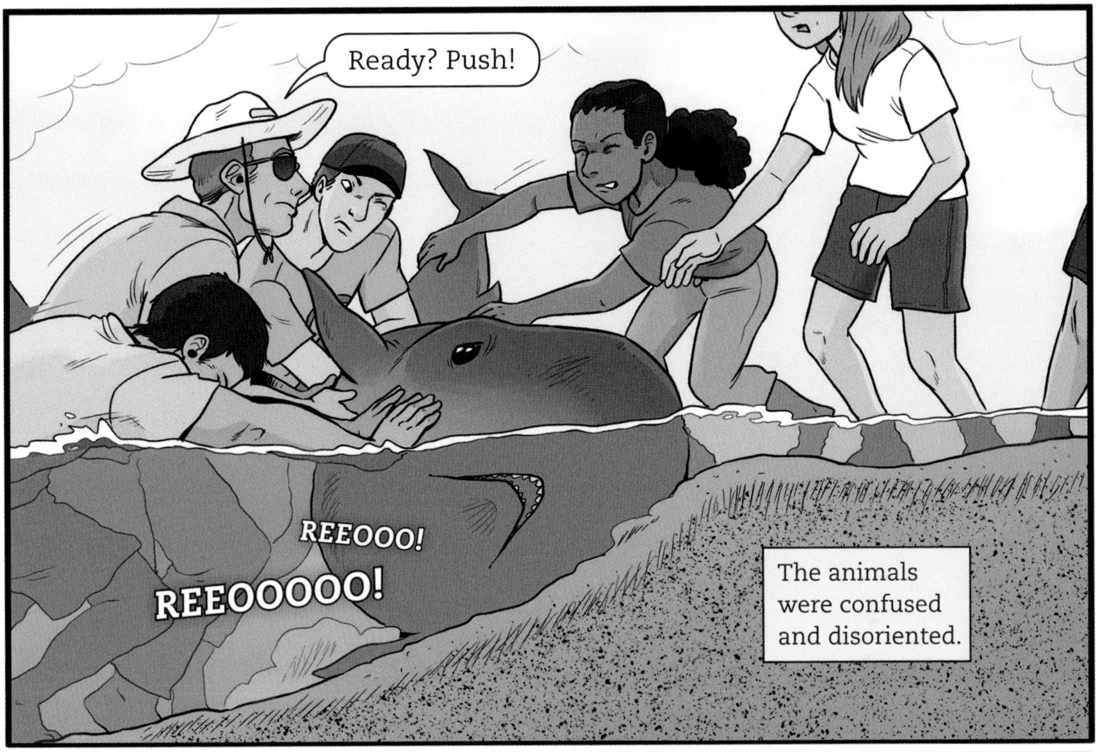
Ready? Push!
REEOOO!
REEOOOOO!
The animals were confused and disoriented.

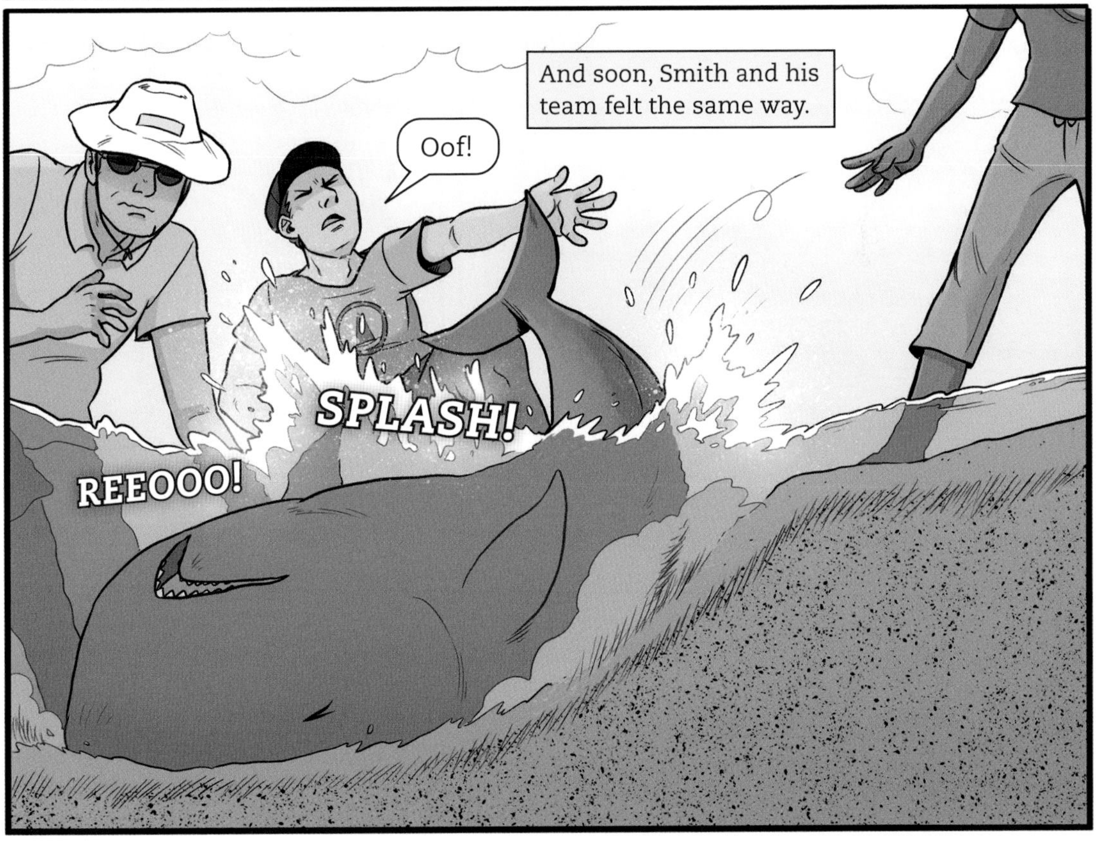
And soon, Smith and his team felt the same way.
Oof!
SPLASH!
REEOOO!

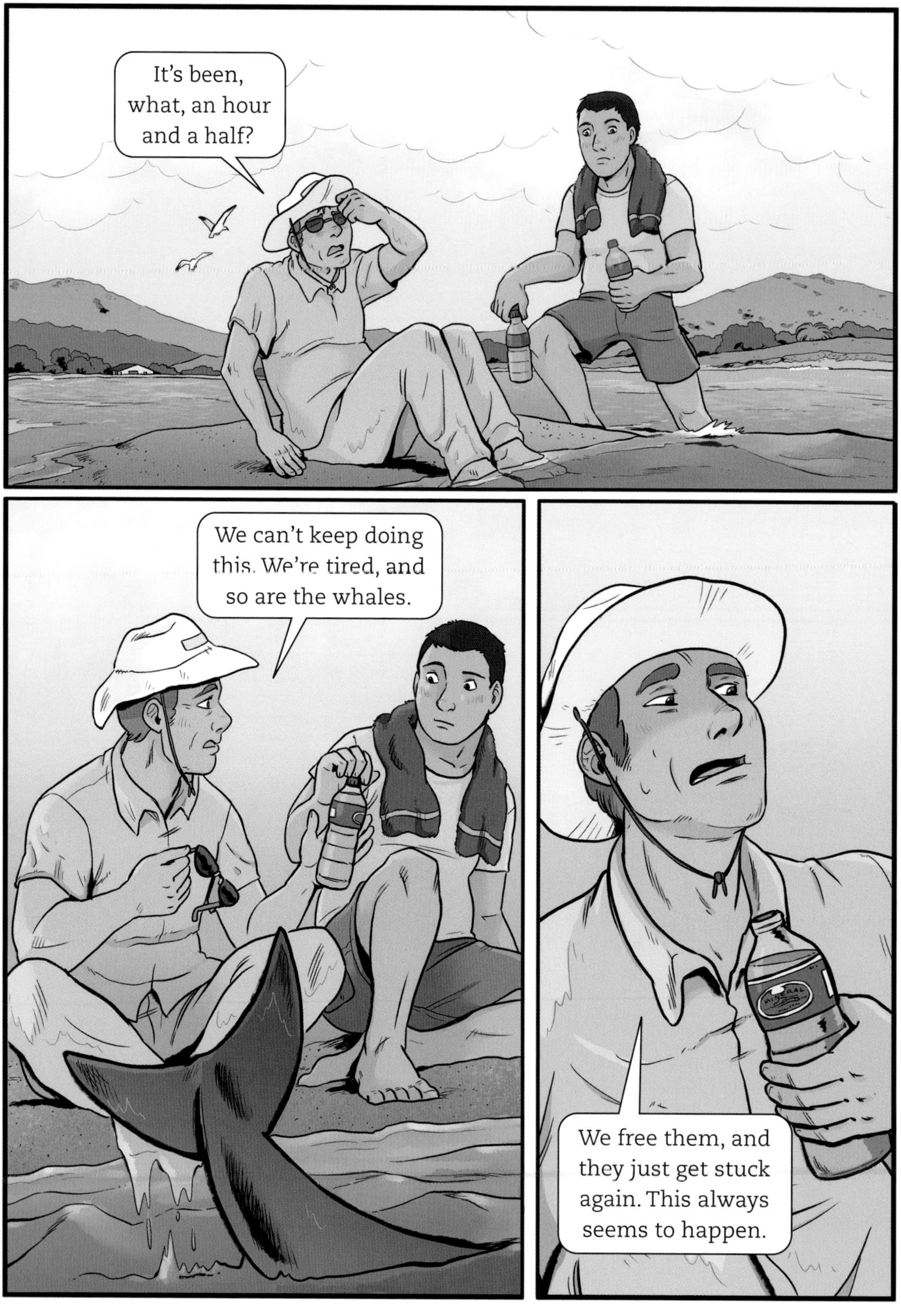
It's been, what, an hour and a half?
We can't keep doing this. We're tired, and so are the whales.
MINERAL
We free them, and they just get stuck again. This always seems to happen.

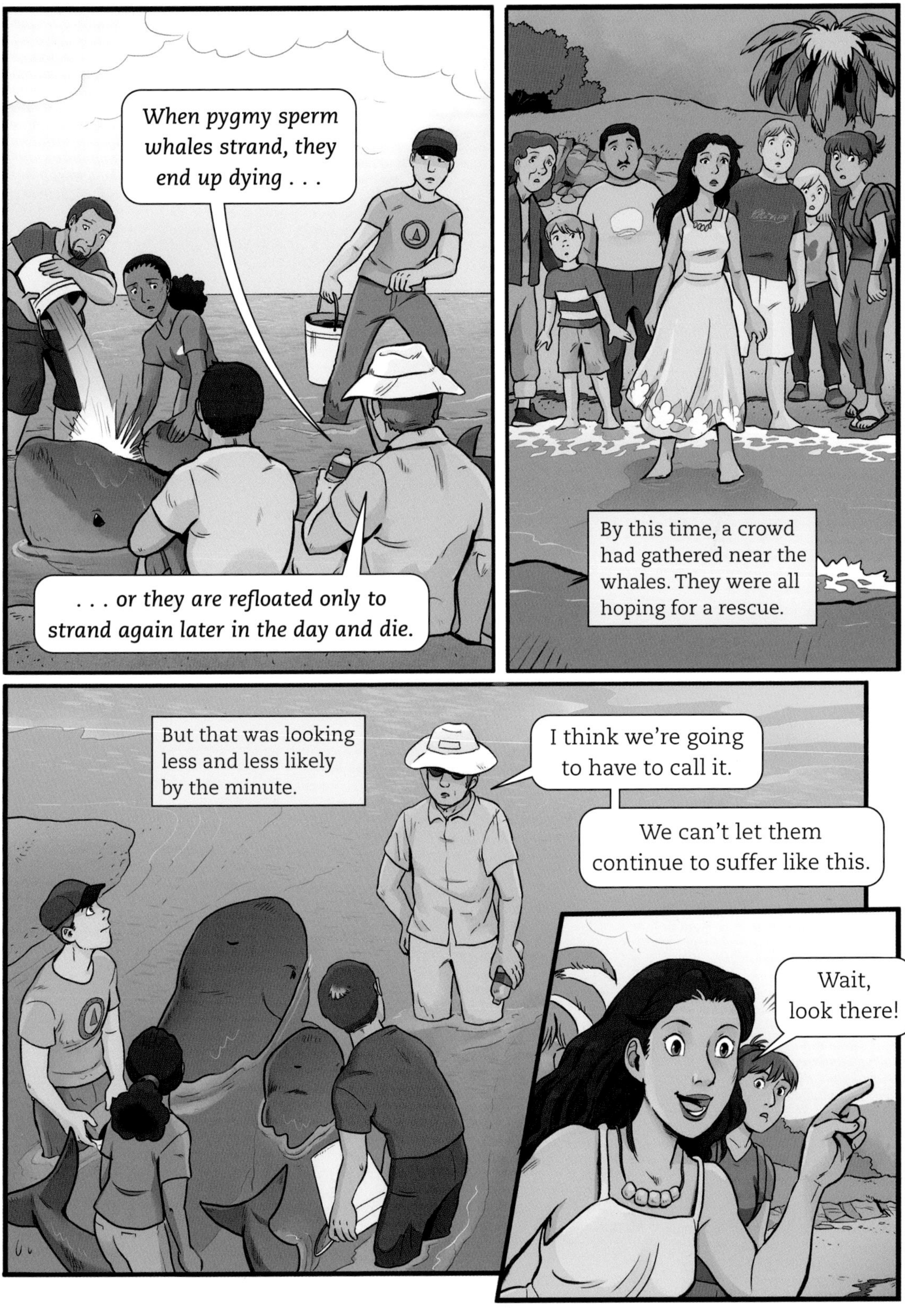
When pygmy sperm whales strand, they end up dying . . .
. . . or they are refloated only to strand again later in the day and die.
By this time, a crowd had gathered near the whales. They were all hoping for a rescue.
But that was looking less and less likely by the minute.
I think we're going to have to call it.
We can't let them continue to suffer like this.
Wait, look there!

Chapter 4: Moko to the Rescue

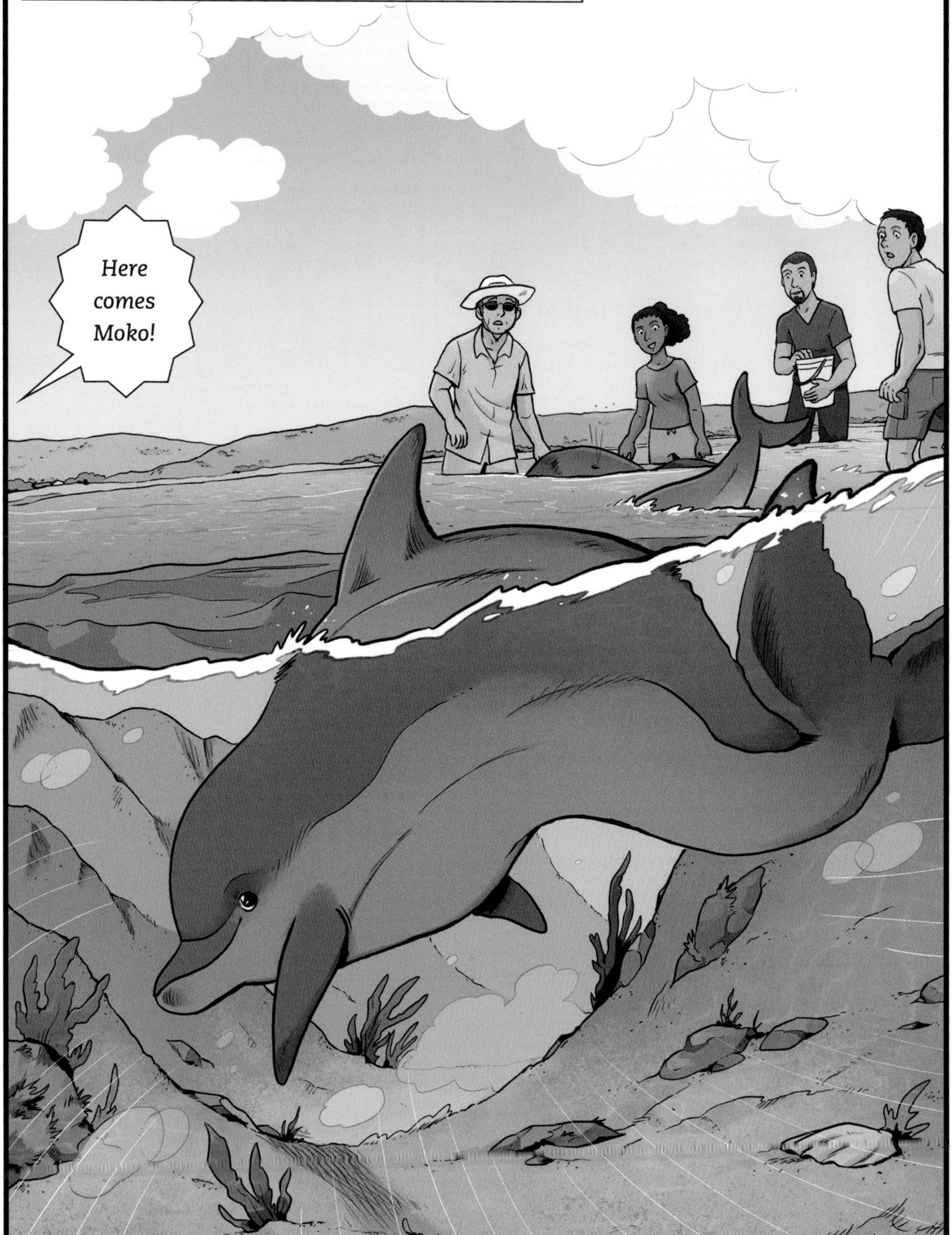
Here comes Moko!

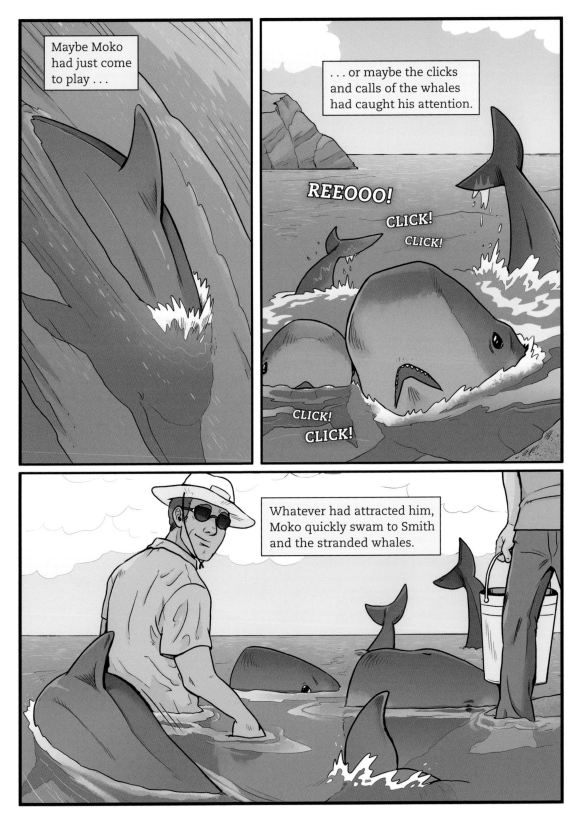

Maybe Moko had just come to play . . .

. . . or maybe the clicks and calls of the whales had caught his attention.

REEOOO!

CLICK!

CLICK!

CLICK!

CLICK!

Whatever had attracted him, Moko quickly swam to Smith and the stranded whales.

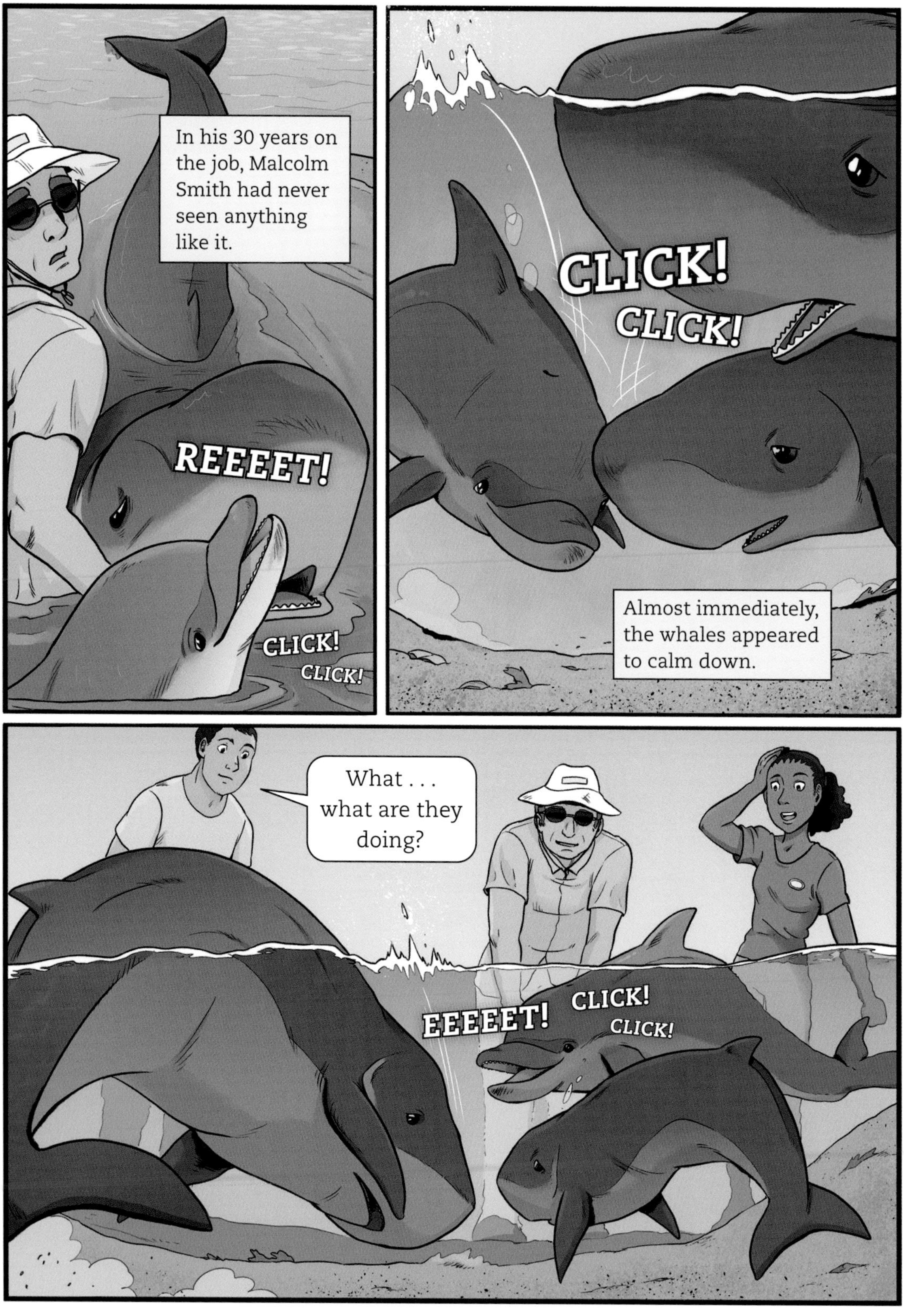
In his 30 years on the job, Malcolm Smith had never seen anything like it.
REEEET!
CLICK!
CLICK!
CLICK!
CLICK!
Almost immediately, the whales appeared to calm down.
What . . . what are they doing?
EEEEET!
CLICK!
CLICK!

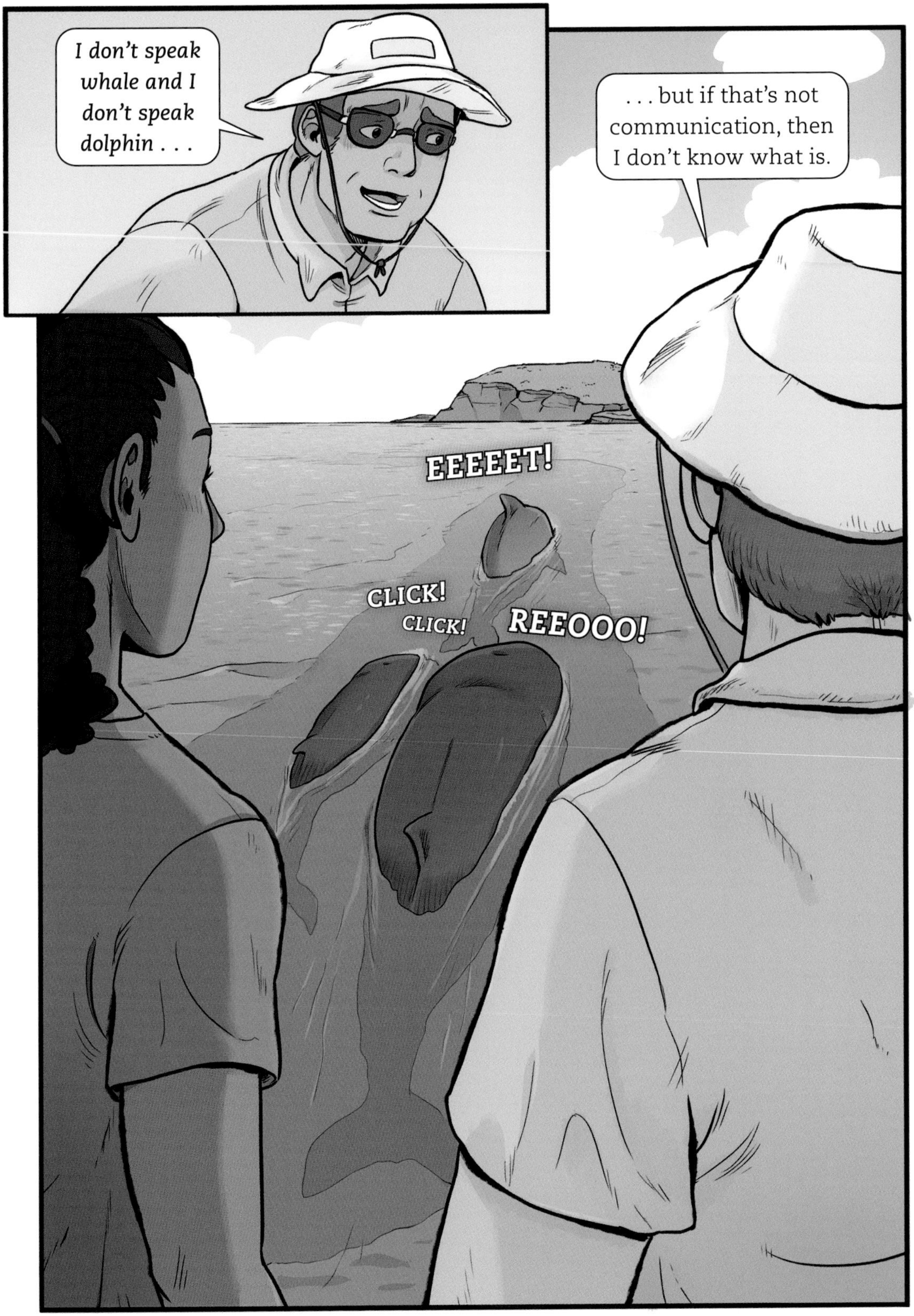
I don't speak whale and I don't speak dolphin . . .
. . . but if that's not communication, then I don't know what is.
EEEEET!
CLICK!
CLICK!
REEOOO!

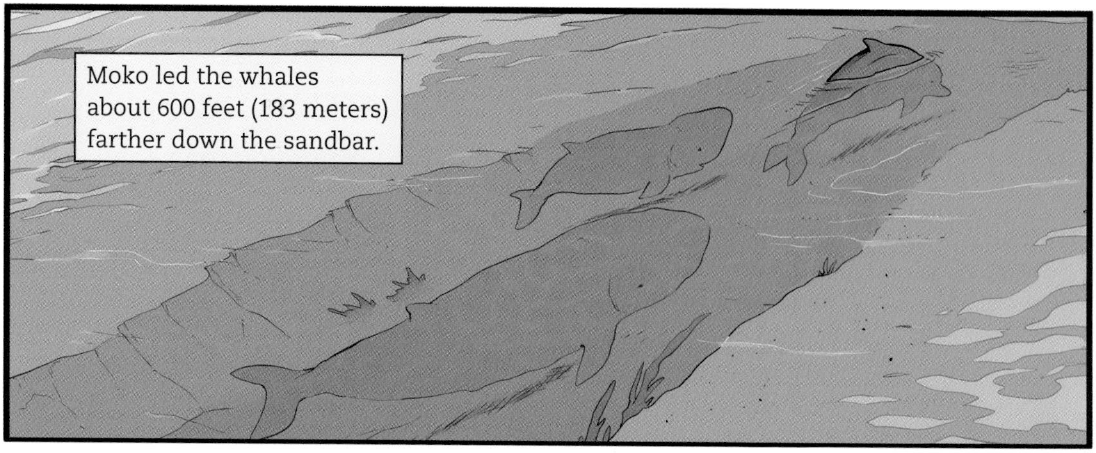
Moko led the whales about 600 feet (183 meters) farther down the sandbar.

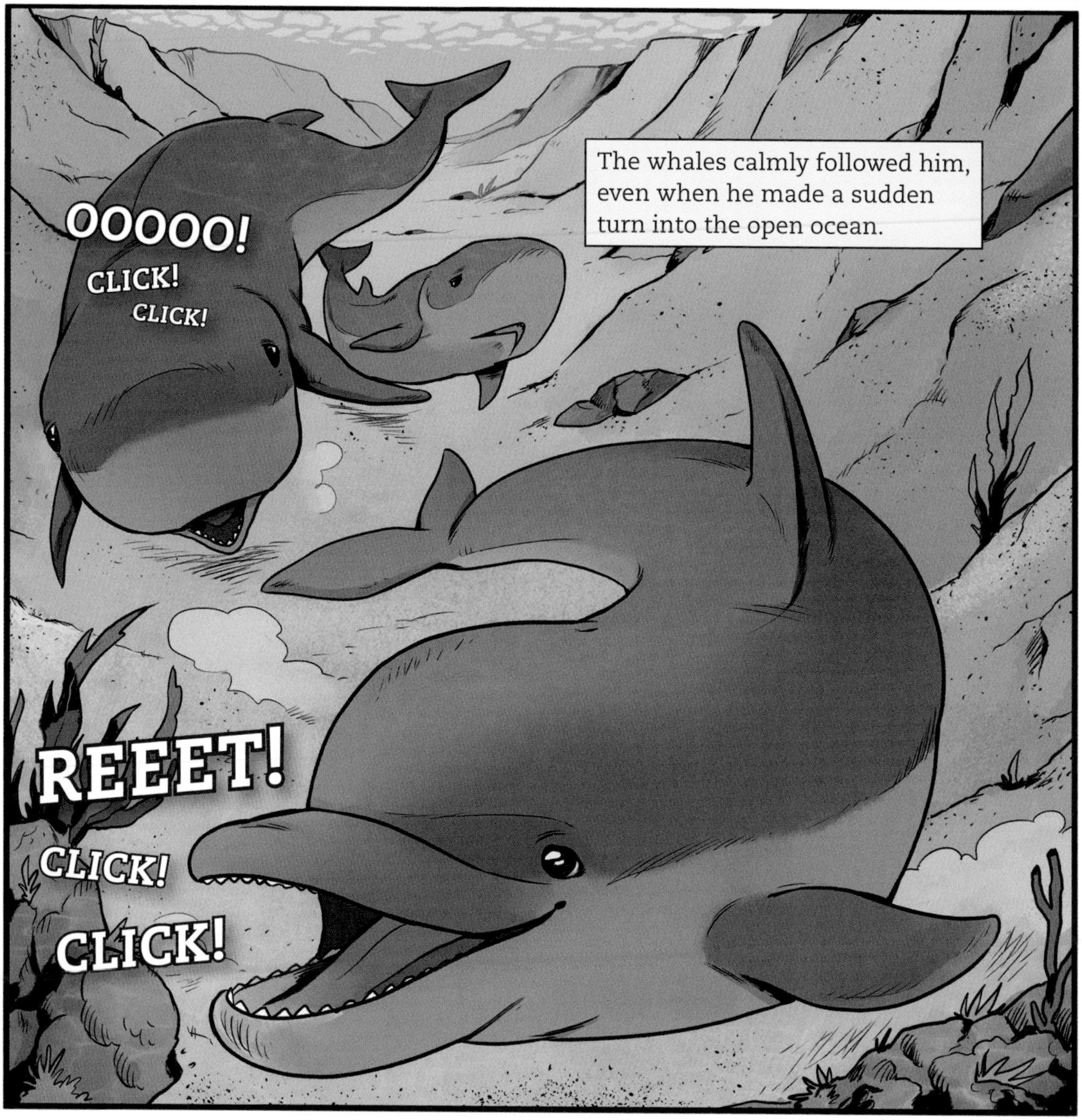
OOOOO!
CLICK!
CLICK!
The whales calmly followed him, even when he made a sudden turn into the open ocean.
REEET!
CLICK!
CLICK!

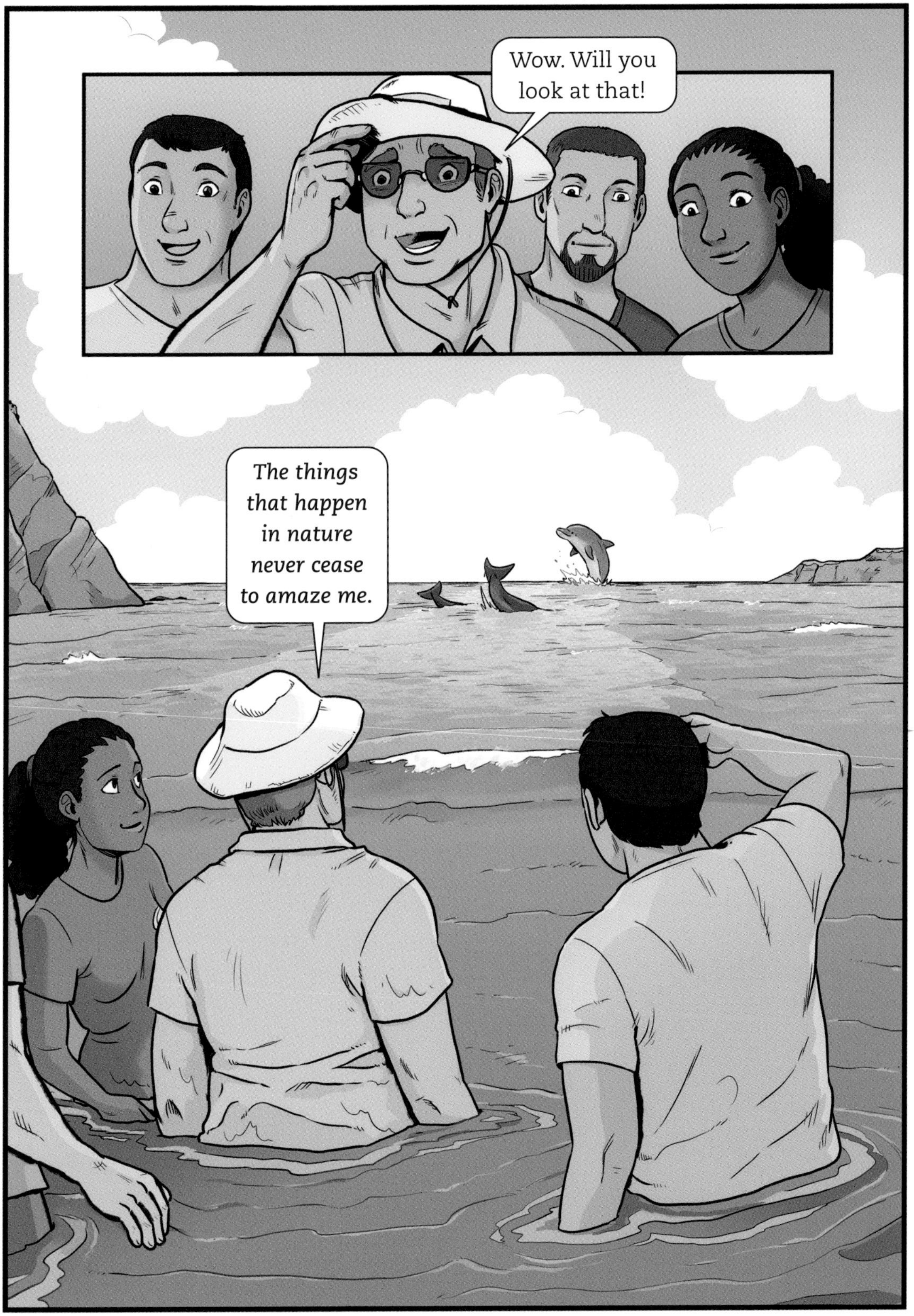
Wow. Will you look at that!
The things that happen in nature never cease to amaze me.

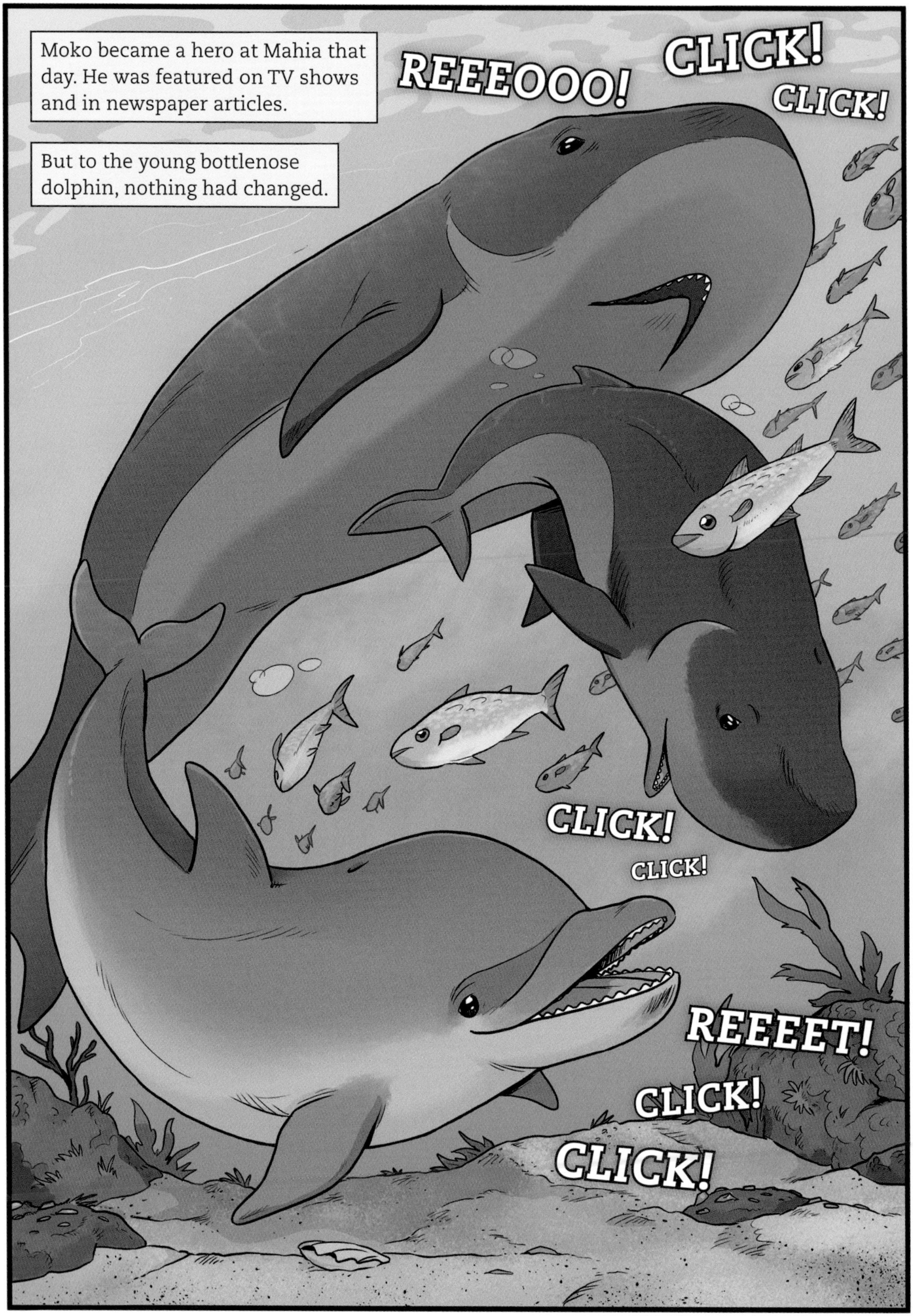
Moko became a hero at Mahia that day. He was featured on TV shows and in newspaper articles.
But to the young bottlenose dolphin, nothing had changed.
REEEOOO!
CLICK!
CLICK!
CLICK!
CLICK!
REEEET!
CLICK!
CLICK!

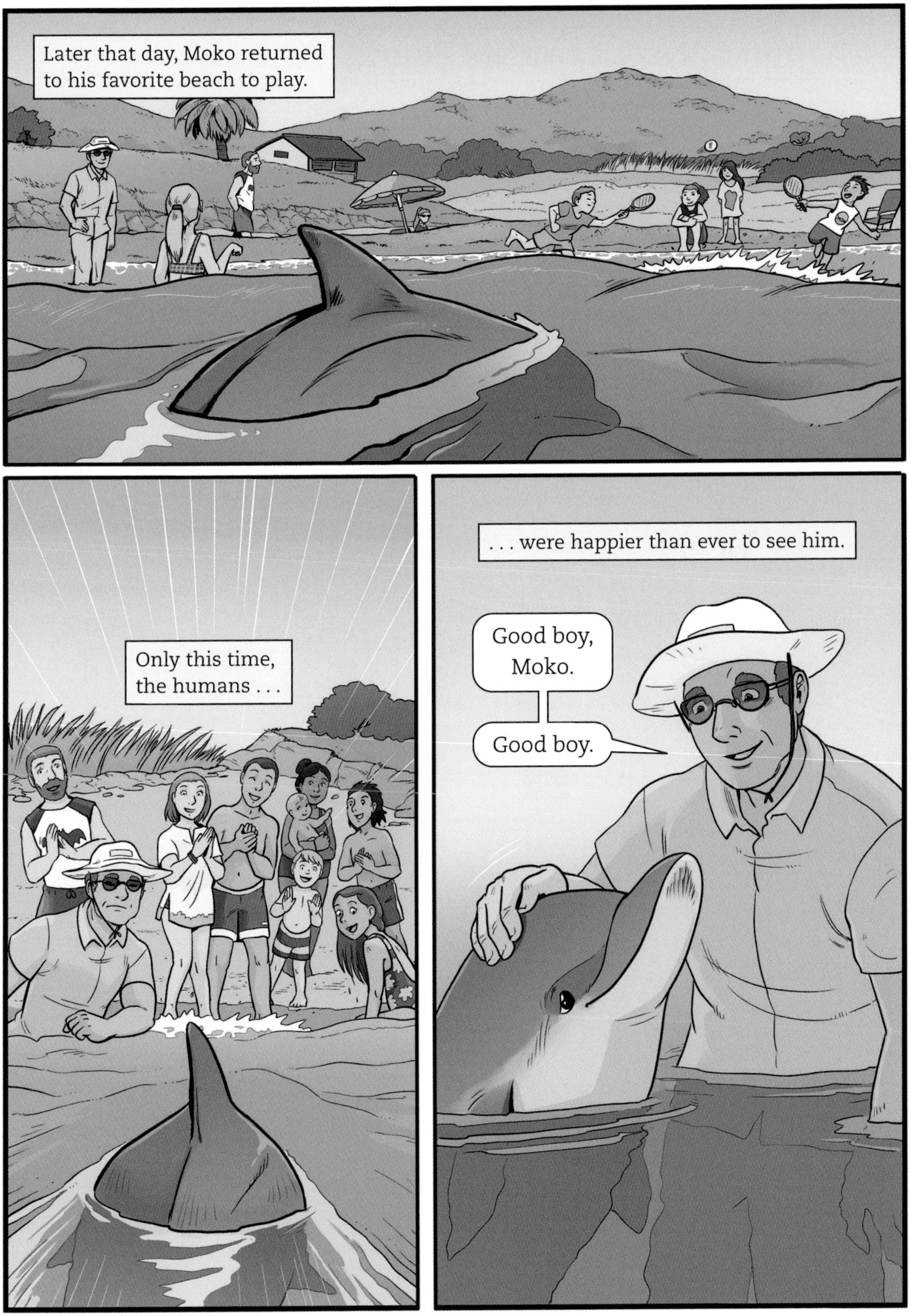
Later that day, Moko returned to his favorite beach to play.
Only this time, the humans . . .
. . . were happier than ever to see him.
Good boy, Moko.
Good boy.

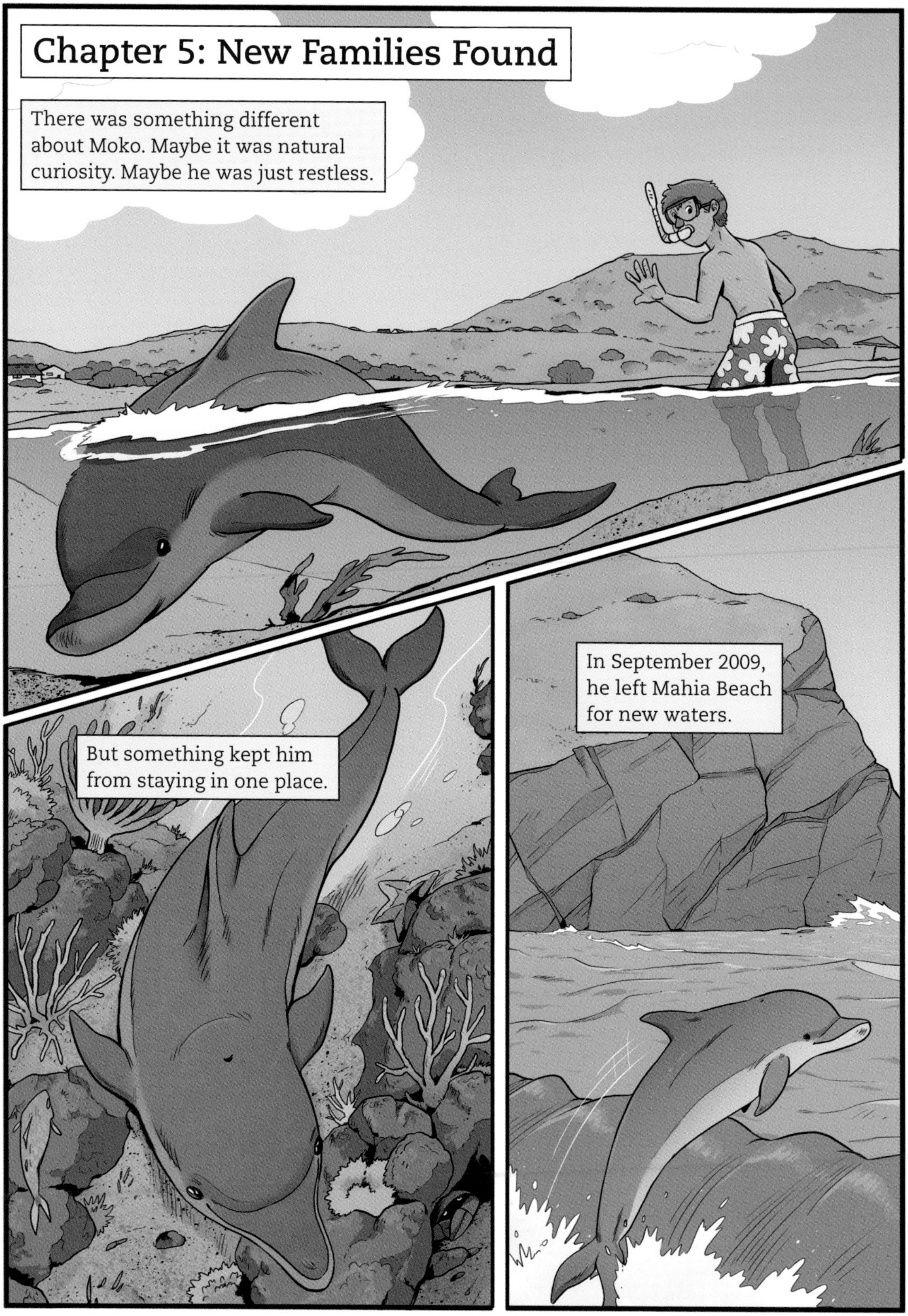
Chapter 5: New Families Found
There was something different about Moko. Maybe it was natural curiosity. Maybe he was just restless.
But something kept him from staying in one place.
In September 2009, he left Mahia Beach for new waters.

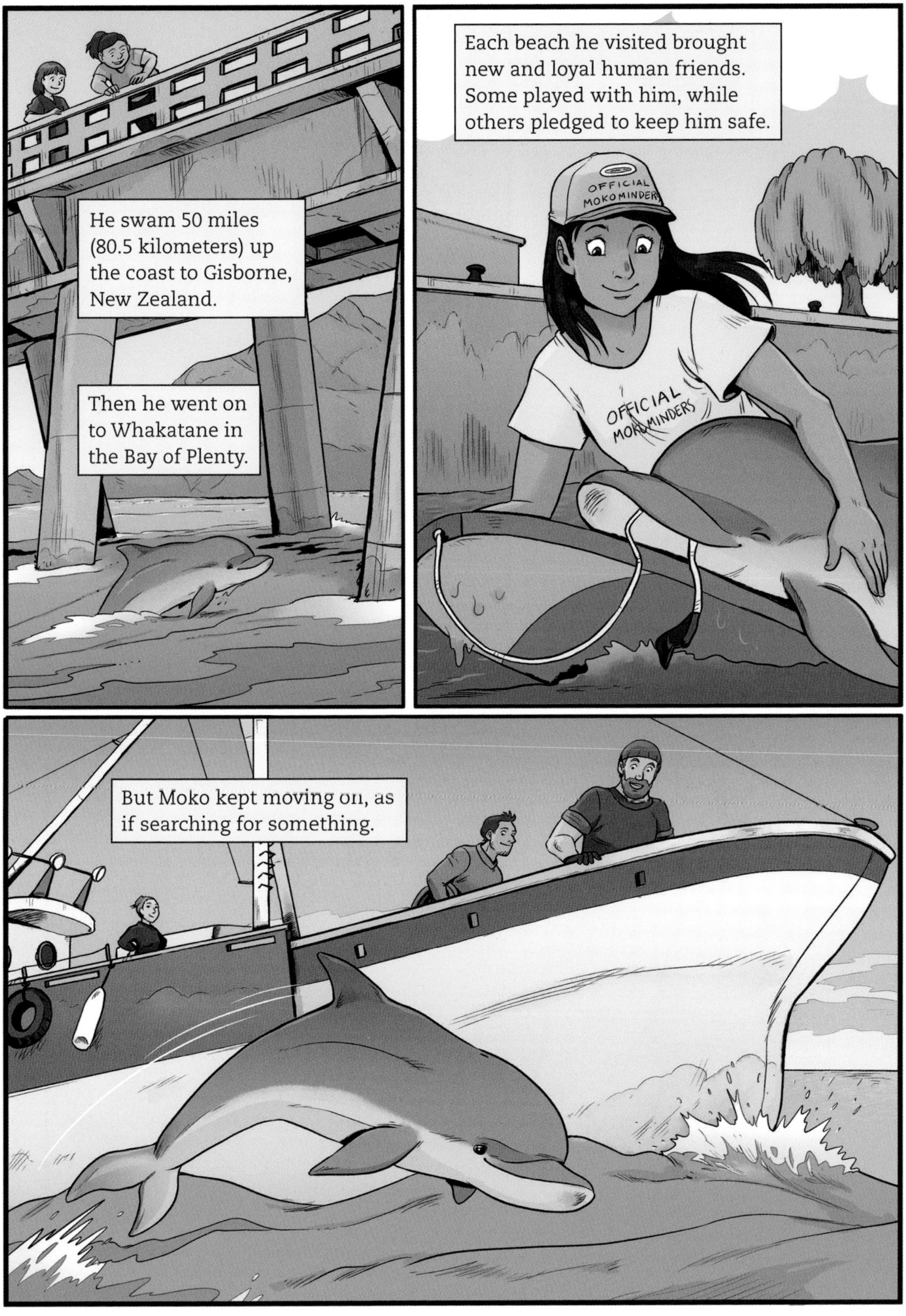
He swam 50 miles (80.5 kilometers) up the coast to Gisborne, New Zealand.
Then he went on to Whakatane in the Bay of Plenty.
Each beach he visited brought new and loyal human friends. Some played with him, while others pledged to keep him safe.
OFFICIAL MOKOMINDERS
OFFICIAL MOKOMINDERS
But Moko kept moving on, as if searching for something.

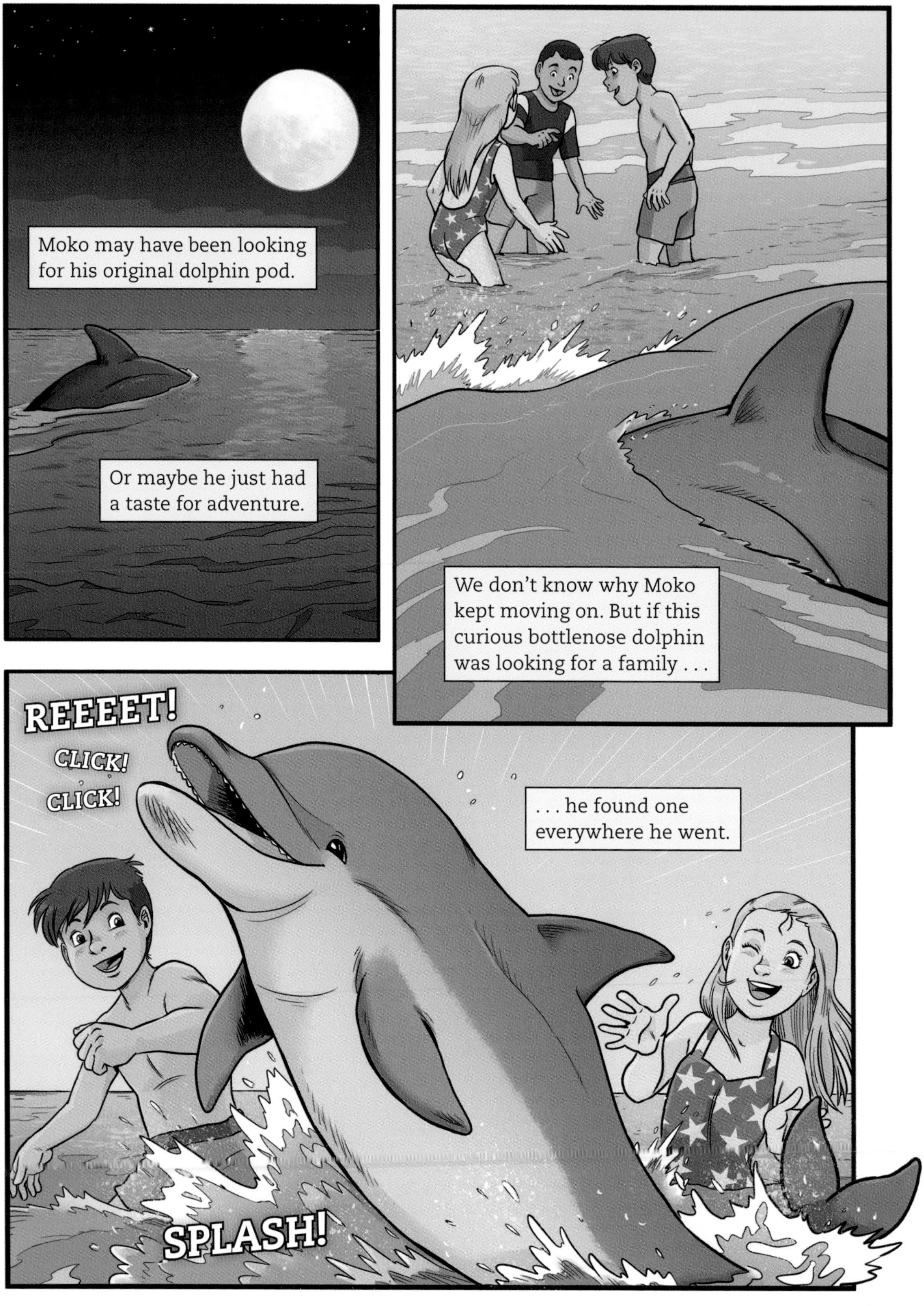
Moko may have been looking for his original dolphin pod.
Or maybe he just had a taste for adventure.
We don't know why Moko kept moving on. But if this curious bottlenose dolphin was looking for a family . . .
REEEET!
CLICK!
CLICK!
. . . he found one everywhere he went.
SPLASH!

Moko's Amazing Life

Bottlenose dolphins can live up to 40 years with their pod. But when separated from its family, a dolphin's lifespan can be much shorter. Unfortunately, in 2010, after wandering to Tauranga, New Zealand, Moko went missing. Two weeks later, his body was found on a nearby beach. He was only about four years old.

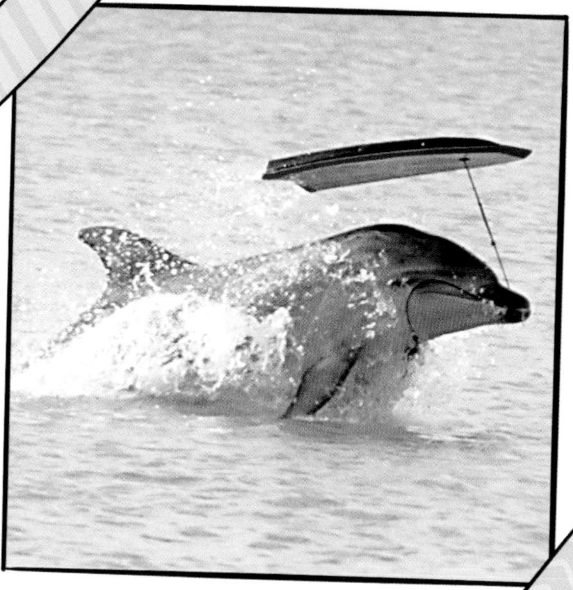

Moko

Although short, Moko's life was amazing. He captured the imagination of New Zealanders and tourists alike. He inspired a children's book, a documentary film, and countless newspaper articles. In 2011, *TIME* magazine included him in their top ten list of heroic animals. Moko will always be remembered as the playful dolphin who saved the lives of two whales and inspired people around the world.

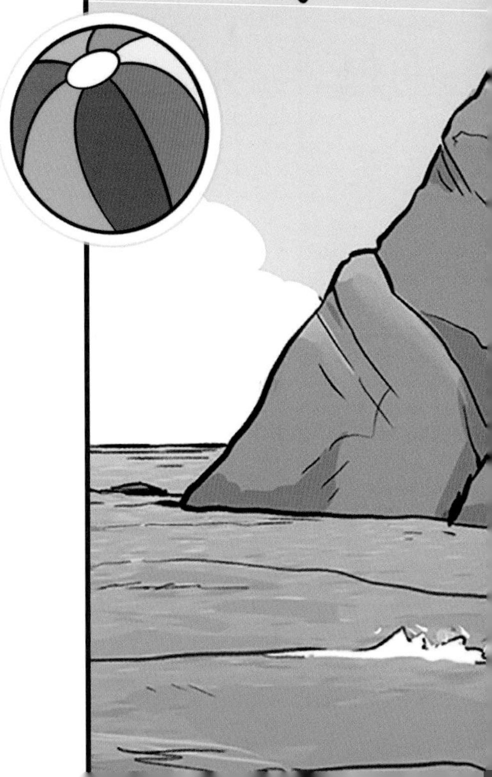

Glossary

affectionate (uh-FEK-shuh-nit) feeling or showing fondness or love for someone

conservation (kon-sur-VAY-shun) the protection of animals, plants, and the natural environment

disoriented (dis-AWR-ee-en-tuhd) to be confused or losing one's sense of direction

pod (POD) a group of whales or dolphins

refloat (ree-FLOAT) to save a marine animal by returning it to open water

restless (REST-lis) unquiet or uneasy; the inability to rest or relax

sandbar (SAND-bar) a ridge of sand in the water near the ocean's shore

tourist (TOOR-ist) a person who travels and visits places for fun or adventure

Read More

Berglund, Bruce. *Togo Takes the Lead: Heroic Sled Dog of the Alaska Serum Run.* North Mankato, MN: Capstone Press, 2023.

Branden, Claire Vanden. *Pink Dolphins.* North Mankato, MN: Capstone Press, 2019.

National Geographic. *125 Animals That Changed the World: Inspiring Tales of Furry Friends and Four-Legged Heroes, Plus More Amazing Animal Antics!* Washington, D.C.: National Geographic Kids, 2019.

Internet Sites

Top 10 Heroic Animals
content.time.com/time/specials/packages/article/0,28804,2059858_2059863_2060210,00.html

Moko the dolphin
whakatane.info/business/moko-dolphin

About the Author

Photo courtesy of
Dorothy Manning Photography

Matthew K. Manning is the author of over 90 books and dozens of comic books. Some of his favorite projects include the popular comic book crossover *Batman/Teenage Mutant Ninja Turtles Adventures* and the 12-issue series *Marvel Action: Avengers* for IDW, *Exploring Gotham City* for Insight Editions, and the six-volume chapter book series Xander and the Rainbow-Barfing Unicorns for Capstone. Manning lives in Asheville, North Carolina with his wife, Dorothy, and their two daughters, Lillian and Gwendolyn. Visit him online at www.matthewkmanning.com.

About the Illustrator

Dolo Okecki was born and raised in Buenos Aires and always loved to draw. As a teen she took an animation course where she discovered the basics of cartooning. After art school and working in studios, she took the leap into illustration and comics! She has illustrated graphic novels, books, and magazines as well as her own graphic novel *Luka's Journey* and one of Capstone's Courageous Kids titles.